Original title:
Ocean's Edge

Copyright © 2025 Creative Arts Management OÜ
All rights reserved.

Author: Elliot Harrison
ISBN HARDBACK: 978-1-80581-703-1
ISBN PAPERBACK: 978-1-80581-230-2
ISBN EBOOK: 978-1-80581-703-1

The Last Light of Day

Seagulls squawk with a goofy cheer,
A sunset dance we hold so dear.
The crabs in tuxedos strut with pride,
While beach balls bounce, taking a ride.

Flip-flops slapping on sandy ground,
Sunburned noses abound all around.
Ice cream dribbles, a sticky delight,
As laughter echoes into the night.

Coastal Reveries

A starfish winks with glee so bright,
While dolphins giggle, oh what a sight.
Buckets and shovels, castles we build,
Yet the tide comes in, our dreams are stilled.

Seagulls swoop down, taking a fry,
We chase them off, oh my oh my!
Umbrellas flipped in a sudden breeze,
Who knew fun could come with such unease?

Faraway Shores and Dreams

On distant sands where flip-flops roam,
We summon mermaids to come home.
With every splash, a silly dance,
The ocean's laughter puts us in a trance.

Sandy sandwiches, tastes quite weird,
With pickles and jelly, the things we feared.
Yet we munch on, with grins so wide,
As surfboards float on the wild tide.

Beneath the Surface

Bubbles rise from a fishy friend,
Who wears a bowtie, don't you pretend!
A treasure chest filled with socks and keys,
What a surprise, we laugh with ease.

Octopuses jive with an awkward flair,
Their eight-legged moves brighten the air.
With giggles echoing through the blue,
Who knew deep down it'd be this true?

Tides Whisper Secrets

The gulls are jesters, squawking loud,
In sandy crowns, they strut so proud.
Crabs in costumes dance a jig,
While fish gossip, 'Is this a big dig?'

Waves tickle toes with slippery grace,
Seagulls steal snacks, oh what a chase!
Starfish lie flat, sunbathing sly,
Reminding us all to just chill and fly.

Lullabies of the Tide

The waves hum tunes, soft and sweet,
While shells keep secrets below our feet.
A turtle dances, slow and grand,
While jellyfish float, trying to land.

The sun dips down, painting the sky,
Crabs throw tantrums, oh my, oh my!
Seashells giggle in the warm sand,
As seaweed sways, a wavy band.

The Call of Distant Horizons

The ship's horn blares, what a loud tune,
While seagulls plot, as cheeky as noon.
A pelican drops, with a splash and a flail,
    Claiming it's just part of his tale!

Sandy toes wiggle, laughter is near,
As beach balls roll, our worries disappear.
A dolphin leaps, what a sight to see,
Making us all laugh, oh joy and glee!

Embracing the Blue

Under the sun, we frolic and play,
With waves that tease, they call us to stay.
A fish in sunglasses flips with flair,
As we wave back, no worries, no care.

Squirt guns blast, and laughter fills air,
As seafoams tickle without any care.
The tide rolls in with a playful nudge,
While we all smile, no need to judge.

A Symphony of Sea Shells

The shells are singing, quite a tune,
With crabs as conductors, under the moon.
A clam's high note, a conch's loud blast,
They play on the shore, a concert so vast.

Seagulls join in, flapping their wings,
Performing a dance, oh, the joy it brings!
While starfish tap dance on the sand,
In this funny show, life is quite grand.

Songs of the Windward Isle

The breeze whispers secrets, a playful affair,
With palm trees swaying, dancing with flair.
A turtle starts rapping, a crab sings the lead,
Here on the sand, where laughter's the seed.

The coconuts giggle, rolling on ground,
While fish in the tide pool jump up and clown.
A parrot squawks loudly, it's quite the surprise,
Who knew that the tropics held such a prize!

Crashing on the Rocks

The waves come tumbling, oh what a show,
They stumble and fumble, then bow down low.
A seaweed wiggle, a barnacle cheer,
As they crash on the rocks, let's all give a cheer!

A dolphin arises, with a splash and a flip,
While sea urchins giggle, not missing a trip.
Here comes a wave, oh what a sight,
Turning the shore into pure delight!

Reflections in the Tide Pools

In shallow waters, the drama unfolds,
With minnows in costumes, they're brave and bold.
Anemones wave, like they're at a ball,
While octopuses ponder, will they dance at all?

A hermit crab shimmies, seeking new style,
Trading shells with a wink, it's done with a smile.
The seaweed twirls, in a swirl of delight,
In tide pool reflections, everything feels right.

Echoes of Distant Shores

Seagulls squawk with jolly cheer,
They steal your fries, oh how sincere.
Crabs in sunglasses move with flair,
Waving claws like they just don't care.

Sandcastles lean, but stand so proud,
Waves rush in, a playful crowd.
Buckets spill with pebbles bright,
As kids squeal with pure delight.

Moonlit Reflections

The moon's a disco ball tonight,
While fish dance under neon light.
Turtles slip on foolish flips,
As jellyfish do the funky dips.

Crabs wear hats that wobble fast,
Marching proudly, they're a blast.
Stars above are jealous, see?
The party here is wild and free!

Dance of the Currents

The tides play tag, with splashes loud,
While dolphins leap and form a crowd.
Fish wearing ties and sneaky grins,
Join in the fun, let's see who wins.

A floating log holds driftwood kings,
They cheer and clash with wooden wings.
Octopus juggles shells with flair,
While seaweed sways without a care.

Call of the Rolling Waves

The waves whisper secrets, hear them cheer,
Wetting our toes, they bring good cheer.
Flip-flops fly with a squeaky squeal,
As beachgoers dash, what a funny deal!

Seashells gossip about fishy tales,
While starfish giggle, waving theirails.
The tide rolls in, what a silly spree,
Collecting laughter, wild and free!

Light Between the Waves

Seagulls squawk like they own the place,
Chasing the waves at a comical pace.
Fish in the water giggle and flop,
While sunburnt tourists just can't seem to stop.

Sandcastles crumble under the sun's glare,
While crabs hold court with a pinch and a stare.
A beach ball escapes like it's got wings,
The laughter rolls in like the tide, and it sings.

Tidal Moods and Melodies

The tide rolls in with a presidential flair,
While jellyfish dance like they just don't care.
Kids with buckets are doing their best,
To capture the magic of the sea's jest.

Seashells whisper tales of days gone by,
As the waves rhythmically wave goodbye.
A picnic blanket keeps blowing away,
And laughter erupts as snacks go to play.

Sketches in Sand

Drawings in sand that the waves can erase,
With squiggly lines in a hapless embrace.
Fortune-tellers read clouds for a thrill,
While surfers yell, 'Lookout!' but it's all just skill.

The sandpiper struts like it's ready to dance,
Tiny footprints vanish with mere happenstance.
A towel gets tangled, a flip-flop takes flight,
While everyone chuckles at the comical sight.

A Meeting of Currents

Fish gossip loudly, a chatty brigade,
While bathers argue over sunscreen shade.
The tides conspire, creating quite the scene,
A crab laughs off questions, makes the water green.

A dolphin leaps out with a splash and a wink,
As beach-goers stare, too stunned to think.
Seagulls stealing snacks, such a daring heist,
At this party of currents, laughter is the spice.

The Rhythm of Nature's Tide

The seagulls squawk in silly ways,
Dancing on air, caught in sun's rays.
A crab in a tux skips by with glee,
Shakes its claws, as if to decree.

The waves come in, and they all retreat,
Only to return for a frothy treat.
A fishy face with a wink and a pout,
Swims in circles, now that's what it's about!

The sun dips down, paints the sky red,
While starfish hold a dance-off instead.
Laughter erupts from the shores all around,
As shells spin tales without any sound.

With a splash and a crash, they make little fuss,
Who knew the brine could be this much plus?
So let's join in this whimsical tide,
Where nature's giggles can never hide.

Forever on the Briny Edge

A dolphin wears shades and flips in the air,
Waving to tourists with a stylish flair.
He hums a tune, oh, what a sight!
Even the sun seems to shine more bright.

Bubbles are blown by a clam with pride,
While a lazy sea turtle takes a ride.
Winking at kids with a slow-motion race,
Saying, "Come on now, let's pick up the pace!"

The tide rolls in, giving sand castles life,
While seagulls plot mischief with much delight.
They swoop and they dive, it's quite the escapade,
As beachgoers giggle, their snacks soon betrayed.

In this world of giggles by the watery bend,
Where every wave brings a story to send.
The briny blue holds a laugh or two,
Forever the jester in nature's grand view.

The Lure of the Abyss

There's a fish with a hat and he swims with glee,
Sipping on jelly, not a care, you'll see.
He tickles the octopus, they dance on the sand,
While crabs throw a party, oh isn't it grand?

The seaweed's a mustache, it sways like a pro,
While dolphins play poker, oh what a show!
The mermaids join in, though their laughs are quite strange,
For their hair is all tangled, oh isn't life change?

Breath of the Sea Breeze

A seagull who sings, thinks he's a diva,
Struts on the shore like a beach party fever.
He steals all the fries and caws with delight,
While pelicans ponder the day in soft flight.

The crabs hold a meeting, decide on a plan,
To take the beach back from this nuisance, the man.
But the tide rolls in, like a sneaky old friend,
And everyone chuckles, the fun never ends!

Island Dreams at Dawn

Palm trees gossip, with coconuts ripe,
As iguanas groove to some weird island hype.
They sip on their smoothies, while turtles just stare,
Wishing they too had a taste of the air.

The sun breaks the horizon like a bright, joyful pie,
While crickets are vibing to the tune of the sky.
A sandcastle stands proud, though it's missing a moat,
As a crab moves in, saying, "Can I be your boat?"

Beneath the Salted Sky

Under the stars, the tide tells a tale,
Of a fish who once dreamed he could fly without fail.
He found a balloon, went up to the clouds,
Said, "Look at me now!" while the fish below crowds.

But the wind blew too hard, and down he did fall,
Right next to a dolphin who laughed at it all.
"Next time," he said, "just stick to the sea,
Where swimming's much easier, come float here with me!"

Guardians of the Coral Reef

In a suit of bright colors, the fish prance,
Grinning at crabs who just can't dance.
They wiggle and jiggle in a coral spree,
Guarding their home, oh what a sight to see!

A turtle with shades glides by the scene,
While a lobster dreams of becoming a queen.
The seaweed sways to a bubbly tune,
As a clownfish laughs at a timid balloon.

Starfish play poker on the ocean floor,
While jellyfish float, what a silly score!
The guard of the reef is a whimsical lot,
All here to create a comedy plot!

Twilight on the Shoreline

The sun sinks low, it's time to unwind,
Seagulls gossip with fishy minds.
Hermit crabs roam with shells in tow,
While sandcastles topple in the flow.

A crab in a tie debates the tide,
While he's trying to keep his pride.
Seaweed tickles a child's toes,
As the tide tickles back with a wave that flows.

Footprints lead to a frisky dog,
Who barks at the waves, a silly slog.
When twilight paints the sky with flair,
Laughter echoes through the salty air.

The Sailor's Heart

A sailor with dreams of winning the race,
Once got lost, looking for his lunch space.
His compass spun, then pointed to fries,
A hungry laugh amidst stormy skies.

He hooted at gulls, they scoffed back with glee,
Dancing on waves, so wild and free.
The anchor's stuck in a pile of seaweed,
His ship's gourmet meal? Just fish-flavored greed!

With a wink to the sea, he starts to sing,
Not a battle cry, but a love song's ring.
He sails off to find the best fishy treat,
With a heart full of laughter and biscuits to eat.

Driftwood Tales

On the shore where driftwood lays,
Funny faces tell tales that amaze.
A stick claims to be an old pirate's rod,
With treasures and secrets, it gives a nod.

A washed-up shoe says, 'I've walked miles!'
While a crab insists he'll run off with style.
Each piece of wood has a wacky story,
In the sunlight, they bask in their glory.

Old bottles whisper of drinks long spent,
As seashells giggle at the time they bent.
Nature's own humor in every grain,
A hilarious gathering without any pain.

Where Water Meets Sky

The seagulls dance in the sun,
With snacks they've stolen for fun.
They squawk like they've hit the jackpot,
As beachgoers laugh at the plot.

Sunburns and sunscreen collide,
With children that giggle and slide.
Sandcastles rise, then they fall,
Kingdoms built for a seagull ball.

The ice cream melts down their hands,
While crabs plot on secretive plans.
Tide pools hide treasures galore,
But the seaweed keeps winning the score.

Beneath the Salted Winds

In flip-flops I'd strut like a star,
But one misstep took me too far.
I tripped on my towel, what a sight,
Flopping around like a fish in flight.

The breeze has a mind of its own,
It flips my hat, I feel overthrown.
With each gust, I chase my own hair,
Like running a race in midair.

Shells whisper secrets from the shore,
While sand gets in places galore.
I laugh at the mess that I made,
Salty and sandy, I'm fully parade.

Glistening Shores at Dusk

The sun dips down like a shy friend,
Colors mix as they start to blend.
With jellyfish lighting the dark,
And fishermen dreaming of a spark.

Coolers pop open with delight,
Where BBQ smoke fills the night.
I burn the burgers, oh what a shame,
But the laughter just fuels the game.

Tide pools reflect the day's last glow,
While starfish share tales that they know.
A picnic's a feast if you drop it right,
Who knew sandwiches could take flight?

Waves of Forgotten Dreams

The surfboards clash in a grand parade,
While sharks contemplate their next charade.
Pro surfers ride with glee and flair,
While I just pray to stay out of the air.

In flippers and goggles, I look real cool,
Yet fall on my face like a sea-washed fool.
With a splash that could scare off a whale,
My skills could use a bit more detail.

The dolphins laugh and high-five each wave,
While I look for something to save.
A beach day's a carnival of fun,
With every flop, there's still a pun.

Serenity on the Coastline

Waves giggle as they race,
Footprints vanish without a trace.
Seagulls squawk in silly glee,
Stealing fries when you decree.

Shells wear hats and dance around,
Crabs doing limbo on the ground.
Turtles wearing shades so cool,
Making beach days feel like school.

Buckets full of frosty treats,
Sandcastles wobble, oh such feats!
Sunscreen slathered everywhere,
Looks like lotion's in my hair.

The breeze whispers jokes so light,
Chasing kites takes flight at night.
Sunburned noses, laughter spills,
At the coast, we forget our drills.

Echoes of the Sea Breeze

The wind whispers, 'Catch your hat!'
A clever crab gives it a pat.
Kids chase waves with squeals of joy,
The tide just washed away their toy.

Jellyfish bob like balloons,
Splashing water, singin' tunes.
Seagulls cheer for stale old bread,
As surfers dream of catching red.

A clam rolled over, sent a text,
'Weekend plans? You'll be perplexed!'
With sand in places quite absurd,
The jokes just keep on being heard.

The sun dips low, what a sight,
Sand in toes feels just so right.
Giggles echo through the night,
As stars above begin to bite.

Dance of the Falling Sun

Dancing shadows chase the beams,
Sunsets paint with sassy themes.
Flip-flops fly in a hopping race,
To catch the light, they must embrace.

Pirates toast with coconut drinks,
While fish swim by and give us winks.
Mermaids giggle, steal the scene,
As we all yell, "What's that sheen?"

The glow reflects on every wave,
Even clams look bold and brave.
The sun slips down without a fuss,
Paddleboards just ride the bus.

As darkness falls, we tell tall tales,
About the brave who sailed with snails.
Laughter rings beneath the sky,
As loopy dreams begin to fly.

Tranquil Depths Beneath

Bubbles rise from fishy chats,
As seaweed sways like funky hats.
Octopus plays games of charades,
While crabs throw parties in the shades.

The schools of fish rush like a train,
Dodging sea stars that look insane.
Anemones dress up in frills,
Collecting laughter with their skills.

Well, squids are painting with their ink,
Creating works while we all wink.
The dolphins dance, a frolic spree,
Popsicles for all, you'll agree!

But wait! A whale sings with a grin,
While jellyfish drift, their under skin.
The depths are filled with joyful sounds,
Where funny antics know no bounds.

Tides of Time

The tide came in, a wave of bliss,
A crab in a tux was hard to miss.
He danced and pranced with utter glee,
While seaweed giggled, oh can't you see?

The seagulls squawked, a wild tune,
As fish threw parties 'neath the moon.
A dolphin in shades tried to surf,
While clams critiqued from their cozy turf.

Bubbles floated, a bubbly mess,
As starfish argued who wore the best dress.
The jellyfish jived, popped like confetti,
In this watery world, oh how it's petty!

The tide rolled back, the laughter soared,
As all took turns with the surfboard.
In the evening's glow, fun is the theme,
Who knew the sea was such a dream?

Echoes of the Deep

Bubbles burst with silly sounds,
As fish chased their fins around.
A turtle sneezed, oh what a sight,
While barnacles giggled at his plight.

The octopus served up some good fries,
While mermaids snorkeled 'neath the skies.
With a flip of a fin, they danced with flair,
Where sea cucumbers couldn't help but stare!

A sunken ship turned into a stage,
As crabs performed, each with a page.
The deep blue held secrets and cheers,
As waves tickled the sand with years.

Echoes rang of playful delight,
Where sea creatures played into the night.
With laughter bubbling like a cool breeze,
Who knew the deep could be such a tease?

Spray of the Setting Sun

The sun dipped low, a painter's brush,
While whales splashed in a joyful rush.
A pelican pranced with a fishy prize,
And the sharks all chuckled at their size.

Gulls played tag through the crimson skies,
While clams sang ballads, much to our surprise.
Seashells juggled in a salty breeze,
As snails debated their speed with ease.

A crab in shades was the trendy king,
Waving his claw, he made the scene swing.
With squawks and laughter, the show went on,
Until the last light of day had gone.

The spray of laughter filled the air,
As waves danced lightly without a care.
What a spectacle, wild and fun,
At the closing act of the setting sun!

Charting the Unknown

With a map made of seaweed and dreams,
We sailed on boats of paper seams.
Crabs held compasses upside down,
As the fish rolled laughing, wearing a crown.

The stars were guides, shining bright,
While seagulls debated the best flight.
With a splash and a pop, we found our way,
In this silly realm where sea critters play.

A treasure chest filled with shells and giggles,
As otters performed their own silly wiggles.
No X marked the spot, just a heap of fun,
Exploration was best when we all could run!

So here we roam, in this watery bliss,
With laughter and joy in every twist.
Charting our course where the fun won't cease,
Where the sea sets the stage for our inner peace!

Sailor's Soliloquy

Oh, the sea's a wobbly friend,
With waves that spin and bend.
My boat's a dance floor on the foam,
Where pirates sing, 'This is home!'

Seagulls squawk their tales of gold,
While my secret stash gets cold.
I blame the fish for all the stink,
But I'm the one who tried to drink!

Tangled nets and knots galore,
With tangled hair I can't ignore.
A mermaid laughs as I fall down,
I've got more grace than a clown!

Fish, oh fish, with scales like bling,
You tease me with your underwater swing.
I'll catch you someday, just you wait,
Until then, I'll blame my fate!

Secrets of the Deep Blue

In depths where sunlight's scared to go,
I met a crab who stole my toe.
He winked at me with a sideways stare,
And danced with friends, a wild affair!

Octopuses play poker in a reef,
While I tripped over seaweed, what grief!
They giggle as I pout and frown,
With eight arms, they'd win my crown.

A dolphin dared me to a race,
But I got lost—what a disgrace!
He flipped and twirled, I splashed around,
He won, and I just made a sound!

Secrets swirl like bubbles bright,
Underwater disco, oh what a sight!
I'll stick to sandcastles, thank you very much,
I'm way too clumsy for the crabby touch!

Between Sand and Sea

Where grains of gold meet waves of blue,
I lost a sandal, oh what to do?
The tide snickered, ran up to tickle,
And here I am, what a sad pickle!

Children build towers, so proud and grand,
While I fight off the gulls with a hand.
They swoop and dive, what a wild chase,
I think I just threw sand in my face!

Seashells whisper their stories dear,
I just want ice cream and some cold beer.
Here comes a wave—goodbye to my book,
Guess it's time for another look!

Squeaky clean in salty air,
I find a crab with a questionable flair.
We form a band—crustacean groove,
Together we make the sand dunes move!

The Tempest's Lullaby

The wind's a jester, howling loud,
With stormy tides that draw a crowd.
Thunder claps like a round of applause,
While I write songs on soggy straws!

Raindrops dance, a tap-tap beat,
Nature's band can't be discreet.
I tip my hat, and take a bow,
To Mother Nature, fierce and wow!

Lightning flashes, oh what cute fright,
I hope it doesn't ruin my night.
The sprinkle of chaos, a splash and a clap,
I'm tucked in my boat, on a giant nap!

So sing along, dear stormy skies,
With whispers sweet and wild surprise.
When this tempest slumbers, I'll rise with glee,
And tell the tales of the raucous sea!

Memory of the Lighthouse Beam

The light spins 'round, all bright, all clear,
Guiding lost boats with a wink and cheer.
It's like a giant flashlight on the sea,
Saying, "Stay away from that old tree!"

With each blink, the sailors laugh and shout,
"Hey, look! There's a beacon, not a trout!"
The gulls glide in, with a squawk and a tease,
Stealing the fries from our sandy knees.

Oh, how the waves giggle and play,
Splashing our toes in a messy ballet.
As the sun dips low, the shadows grow long,
One last giggle in this seafaring song.

Baiting the Hook

With a worm on a hook, we set our plan,
To catch the big one, yes, that's the man!
But the fish just laugh and swim right by,
 "We've seen that bait! It's a clever lie!"

The crab sidesteps, with a claw in the air,
 "Sorry, old chum, but we just don't care!"
While the seagulls swoop with their beady eyes,
 "Fresh fries or fish? You'll be our prize!"

We chat and we chortle, not caring at all,
As the sun starts to set and the night starts to call.
Casting our lines, it's more comedy gold,
 Than catching fine fish that's ever been told.

In the Wake of Adventure

Here comes the boat, let the fun times roll,
But I forgot my hat! Now I'm on a stroll.
The waves lap up, a splash in the face,
"Oh no!" I squeal, as I seek for my place.

The skipper's a joker, with a grin so wide,
"Hold on tight, mate! We're in for a ride!"
But the wake pulls us back, like a clingy friend,
While we giggle and wobble, we're sure to offend!

With each quirky bump, we swing left and right,
Dancing on deck, what a comical sight!
The seafoam's our partner in this silly jig,
As we laugh and we shout, just a bunch of big kids.

Currents of Memory

I remember that day when we built a great fort,
Of driftwood and shells, what a splendid sport!
But the tide crept in, with a chuckle and grin,
"Your castle's now sand, let the water begin!"

We chased the waves, like a game of tag,
With splashes of laughter, all joyful and brag.
Seagulls danced overhead, with their raucous caws,
"Is that a beach picnic or just fish in paws?"

As we tossed our last frisbee toward the blue,
A dolphin leapt up, like, "What's wrong with you?"
With memories swirling in the salty breeze,
Life's funny in moments like these, oh please!

Maritime Mythos

The fish all wear little hats,
Sipping tea on rubber mats.
Octopuses dance in fine ballet,
While seahorses start their cabaret.

A crab complains of tired feet,
Dance recitals can't be beat!
Dolphins juggle glowing balls,
As seaweed claps with leafy thralls.

Even the clams have secret dreams,
Plotting heists, or so it seems.
Mermaids try to run the scenes,
While shrimp just laugh and share their beans.

So when you think the coast is clear,
Remember sea life holds its cheer.
In underwater cafés, tales unfold,
Of pirate jokes forever told!

The Color of the Sea

The waves wear shades of minty green,
And goldfish strut like they're the queen.
With coral reefs providing flair,
Even starfish love a little wear.

Giant squids play peek-a-boo,
While turtles swim in sunglasses too.
Bubbles rise with fizzy pride,
As fish gossip as they glide.

The seabed's bright with tales and dreams,
Of jellyfish in purple creams.
Nautical life in vivid hues,
Makes vivid friendships, not just blues.

So when you dip your toes in tide,
Remember there's bright humor inside.
Where every splash is met with glee,
And every ripple holds a spree!

Where Stars Meet Water

At twilight, fish throw starry raves,
And whales sing tunes from watery caves.
The moon gets jealous, shines so bright,
While crabs jam out all through the night.

Starfish wish upon a wave,
For surfboards made of seaweed brave.
Dolphins pull pranks with a splash,
Watching the seagulls tumble and crash.

Anemones wear glittery crown,
While blowfish puff and spin around.
A charm in the dark, tales are spun,
As jellyfish twinkle, just for fun!

So if you stare at the sky so deep,
Remember the secrets the waters keep.
For laughter bounces, echoes true,
Where stars meet waters in shades of blue!

Tidal Whispers

The tide tickles toes as it retreats,
Making its way with sneaky feats.
Seagulls squawk, like they own the shore,
While crabs debate what they're fighting for.

A sea cucumber starts a scene,
Declaring he's the ocean's king.
The clowns of the deep join the fray,
With jokes that make the dolphins sway.

Mollusks play hide-and-seek all day,
In shells so shiny, bright, and gay.
Water spins tales with each ebb and flow,
Tickling the sand where laughter's aglow.

So next time you're by the watery rim,
Listen closely to the tales within.
Each wave whispers secrets to those who care,
Of humorous hits that dance in the air!

Cradled by the Waves

Seagulls dive, they steal my fries,
I shout, "Hey, no food for the flies!"
Sand castles rise but then they fall,
Tide's got jokes, it loves to sprawl.

Crabs wear hats like tiny kings,
They dance around, it's all good things.
I laugh so hard, I slip and flop,
Anyway, let the beach party pop!

Surfboards wobble, riders squeal,
Waves bring laughs, it's quite the deal.
Splashing kids with squeaky toys,
Who knew the tide could make such noise?

As sunset paints the sky in cheer,
We prance and play, there's naught to fear.
With sandy toes and salty hair,
I'll chase the waves without a care.

Starlit Waters and Shadows

Beneath the stars, my friend's a starfish,
He won't move, oh, what a delish!
We laugh and yell, splash like a whale,
His frozen pose tells quite the tale.

Moonlight dances on jellyfish glows,
I watch them wiggle, strike funny poses.
A fishy prank, a slippery play,
Can't catch a cold when you swim at bay!

With a bucket of clams, we sing and cheer,
The sandworms wiggle, oh dear, oh dear!
Mysterious creatures dance in delight,
Pulling my legs as I take flight.

Through the shadows, a treasure hunt grows,
Gold plastic coins where nobody goes.
We raise our cups of sweet lemonade,
Living it up in this twilight parade!

The Driftwood Chronicles

Once I found a piece of wood,
It looked like a fish—well, sort of good!
I named it Fred, it's quite the champ,
We built him a palace with shells and stamps.

A seagull swooped down, took Fred for a joyride,
I chased it around, oh, what a wild slide!
I tripped on a shell, fell flat on my face,
Fred flew away, with peace and grace.

Driftwood tales and ocean lore,
Who knew this beach could offer more?
With buddies made of stick and sea,
Life's a treasure—come join me!

As night draws near, I clasp my finds,
Seashell treasures, oh, what kinds!
Fred's spirit stays close, even if he's gone,
In my driftwood book, our stories live on.

Crashing Symphonies

Waves collide with a thundering cheer,
Nature's band, right here in the sphere!
Sand drummers pound, seaweed strums,
 Clams join in with their oceanic hums.

Seashells ring like chimes in the breeze,
 I dance along, just doing my tease.
The dolphins play sax, oh what a sight,
Who knew beach bands could rock all night?

Barnacles tap on rocks with flair,
While fish create a splashy affair.
I twirl and whirl, join the grand jam,
Mollusks groove—now that's the plan!

Under the stars, I sing with glee,
The moon's our DJ, setting us free.
With every crash, laughter takes flight,
 Together we sway, till morning light!

Hanging Between Tides

Seagulls squawk with sass today,
As they steal fries and fly away.
My picnic's gone, and all that's left,
Is a sandwich stuck, just like my heft.

The waves roll in with a playful shove,
They splash my shorts, a watery glove.
I try to run, but slip and flop,
The beach folks laugh, I take a drop.

Sunburned noses and silly hats,
I dance around like clumsy chaps.
A crab scuttles past, a judge in court,
And I'm the clown in this seaside sport.

With sand in my toes, I sit in glee,
Waving at fish that swim by me.
In this quirky realm of surf and sun,
Life's a joke, let's all have fun!

The Windswept Promenade

The breeze is wild, it's tousled my hair,
I walk like a penguin, but who would care?
With every gust, my hat's airborne,
Like a balloon, without a mourn.

Tourists shuffle, camera in tow,
Posing by seaweed—what a show!
One slips and falls, a slapstick scene,
In this land where we all feel keen.

Kites spiral high, swirling through blue,
While kids scream loud at the sneaky seagulls, too.
Balloons escape, and suddenly sway,
Chasing sunshine in a fishy ballet.

Churros and sandcastles, a day so bright,
Yet here I am, a fallen sight.
These windswept tales, they tickle my soul,
In this promenade, laughter's the goal!

Reflections on Liquid Glass

The water shimmers, a slippery prank,
I slip as I wave from the sandy bank.
The mirror laughs back with waves of glee,
As fish make faces right back at me.

A child throws in a soda can,
Watch it float, what a brilliant plan!
Mermaids giggle from their secret lair,
While I splash about without a care.

Reflections dance like goofy dreams,
In between the seagull's screams.
I spot a flip-flop, is it mine?
The one that vanished? Now it's fine!

Sunset's here and the jokes are loud,
A beachside audience, oh so proud.
With shadows stretching, we're all aghast,
At the funny faces this day has cast!

Skimming the Surface

I grab my board like a knight with flair,
Trying to surf without any care.
A wave comes crashing—oh what a ride!
I land face first, with pride denied.

Floats and noodles, a carnival sight,
As sunburnt folks splash with delight.
Kids are laughing, making a scene,
While I'm just flailing, a fishy bean.

The lifeguard chuckles, eyeing my fate,
Sipping his drink, oh isn't that great?
I wave my arms like a scarecrow tight,
As beach balls bounce and take flight.

Under the sun, we dance and slip,
In this seaside carnival, let's all dip.
With laughter ringing, we play all day,
At the shore's embrace, come join the fray!

Currents of Change

The fish are having quite the chat,
As bubbles rise from where they sat.
"Do you think we'll catch a break?"
"Nah! Just more seaweed salad to make!"

The crabs all dance in their own way,
Pinching claws to start the play.
"Dance off, who can do a spin?"
"I'll take that bet, let the fun begin!"

Seagulls swoop, they steal a fry,
Then drop it like it's too dry.
"Whoa, I thought it was a treat!"
"Guess they just wanted something sweet!"

Waves crash down with silly splashes,
While jellyfish float with flashy flashes.
"Do you think I'm getting older?"
"Nah, just a bit more of that salty cold water!"

Dusk Over the Horizon

The sunset stains the sky so red,
A fish jokes, "I just want bread!"
"Not fishy bread, I want the good!"
"Tough luck, here's some seaweed food!"

A turtle ambles at a slow pace,
"I might just win the great sea race!"
His friends all laugh, they start to cheer,
"Let's make you fast with a salty beer!"

Starfish play cards on a rock,
"Hey, it's my turn, don't you mock!"
With every flip, they laugh and pout,
"I'm the best, there's no doubt!"

As twilight paints the world anew,
A dolphin adds, "What's wrong with you?"
They all just grin, it's time to soar,
"Let's dive tonight, who knows what's in store?"

Surrender to the Depths

A crab declared, "I'm off to hide!"
"Why?" asked a clam right by his side.
"Because the fish think I'm a snack!
And I just want my shell to crack!"

A snail mumbled, "I'm going slow,"
"I'll just take a look at the flow."
His friend said, "Dude, pick up the pace!
Or you'll be lost in this crazy race!"

A shark swam by, with silly flair,
Bumping into a soft sea hair.
"Oops, pardon me!" he gave a grin,
"Just passing through, let the fun begin!"

Then came a whale with a giant splash,
Said, "Sorry folks, just had a crash!"
They all just roared with laughter loud,
"Surrendered to the fun, not the crowd!"

Mists of the Morning Sea

In morning mist, the crab sings sweet,
"Why did I cross this slippery street?"
"Don't slip, it's just a little dew!"
The starfish giggled, "Look at you!"

A sea otter rolls with a fishy grin,
"Who knew breakfast could be such a win?"
"Just don't forget to share the bait,
Or breakfast club might seal your fate!"

The seabirds squawk in playful glee,
"Did we miss the best jam at sea?"
"We'll spread it thick, we've got the crust,
With laughs and fun, just think we must!"

As sun breaks through the morning haze,
The ocean sparkles in playful rays.
With giggles and gaffs, they sail anew,
"Let's catch the tide and ride this blue!"

A Fisherman's Folktale

There once was a fish wearing a hat,
He claimed he was tough, a real acrobat.
When tossed to the waves, he gave a loud shout,
"I'm swimming away, let me out!"

With a wink and a splash, he did a ballet,
While the fisherman sighed, "It's not a good day!"
With a pole and a line, he set out to catch,
But the fish was a dancer, and he couldn't match!

A crab then burst through, with jokes up his sleeve,
"I'm the king of the sea, now that you believe!"
With a pinch and a dance, he stole the show,
While the fisherman laughed, "I'm just here for the taco!"

The waves rolled in, and the sun shone bright,
While the fish did a flip, what a hilarious sight!
The fisherman chuckled, his catch was a joke,
As he cast out again, for another fine poke!

Salty Souvenirs

I wandered the shore for some treasures to find,
But all that I got were some shells, never mind!
A crab waved his claws like he ran a bazaar,
"Buy a trinket or two, just don't take my car!"

A seagull swooped down, grinning wide with glee,
"Steal my fries, and I'll ask for a fee!"
With a flap and a squawk, he flew with a caw,
While I searched for some pearls in the sand and the straw.

The tide rolled back, and I noticed a shoe,
One that was bright, with a wild shade of blue!
"Salty souvenir, fit for the dance,
I'll wear it with pride and take it to France!"

A starfish then giggled, with a smile so chic,
"My friends call me Larry, let's party this week!"
As the sun set low, and the waves sang along,
We laughed through the night, with the tide as our song.

The Treasure Beneath

Down in the depths where the mermaids sing,
Lies treasure galore, oh what a bling!
But the octopus guard has a terrible thrust,
"No treasure for you, it's covered in rust!"

With eight arms flailing, he danced a fine jig,
While the goldfish just chuckled, "What a big swig!"
"Hey, friends!" called a clam with a mischievous wink,
"Let's hide all the spoils, then take a quick drink!"

The treasure chest opened, it creaked and it groaned,
With coins that were coated in seaweed and foam.
"Arr, here's my loot, come and join in the fun!"
As the fish had a party, under tides barely spun.

But a whale came along, with a splash and a roar,
"Are you all having fun? Come and dance on the shore!"
With bubbles and laughter, the crew made a scene,
While the octopus laughed, "Who knew it was keen!

Search for the Horizon

With a map made of jelly and a boat made of bread,
I sailed with a parrot, who mistook me for thread!
"Off to the horizon, where dreams blend and swirl!"
As he flapped his bright wings, giving quite the twirl.

The waves laughed and whispered, with a tickle and tease,

"What do you seek? A treasure or cheese?"
With a wink and a splash, I searched for a prize,
But all I found back was a crab with big eyes!

The journey went on, and the sun climbed high,
As I tossed out a snack, hoping not to dry.
But the seagulls showed up, like a feathery fleet,
"We came for the crumbs, this bread is a treat!"

The parrot just cawed, summoning flair,
"Where is the treasure? It can't be out there!"
But the horizon grew near, in a dance of great grace,
With laughter and joy filling up all the space.

Over the Stormy Waters

Waves are jumping like a pogo stick,
Seagulls squawking, oh what a trick.
Sand is flying, making quite a mess,
And here I am, in my Sunday best.

A crab approaches, wearing a hat,
I laugh and say, 'Now, isn't that fat?'
He pinches my toe, it's quite a surprise,
I run like the wind, oh how time flies!

The boat's doing spins like a ballerina,
Captain's yelling, 'A storm is a-leanin!'
But I just sit back with my soda pop,
And watch the waves as they flip and flop.

A dolphin jumps in a tuxedo fine,
I cheer him on, 'You're one of a kind!'
The laughter echoes across the bay,
As we dance with the tides, hip-hip-hooray!

Cradle of the Dunes

In the sand hills, kids play hide and seek,
While a pelican tries to sneak a peek.
Buckets and shovels, we build a throne,
Then, a wave comes, and it's all overblown.

A seagull swipes my peanut butter spread,
I shout, 'Not my lunch, you feathered head!'
With a flapping laugh, he takes to the skies,
While I chase him down, surprise in my eyes.

The sandcastle's wonky, a lopsided sight,
But we crown it a king — it's a glorious plight!
Shells piled high like a treasure hoard,
Then, a rogue wave comes, and we're totally floored.

With giggles and splashes, we forget the sun,
This sandy adventure is just too much fun.
As the tide rolls in and the day slips away,
We'll always remember this zany play.

Time Slips Away at Sea

I set my watch to the rhythm of waves,
But time's just a joker, and it misbehaves.
One hour ties up like a ship's knotted sail,
And before I know, I'm stuck in a tale.

Seashells are ticking like clocks on the shore,
I dig for the treasure but find a sore chore.
The waves whispered secrets but took my hat,
Now I'm a sailor with no stylish spat.

With every splash, I lose track of the day,
My drink's gone warm, did I just hear it say?
The sun, it seems, plays a trick on my eyes,
As seagulls conspire with mischievous cries.

"Is it lunch or is it brunch?" I ponder anew,
But the sandwiches float, like birds in a queue.
Days mix with nights, like the foam in the tide,
And laughter's the clock that we cannot abide.

Seahorse Dreams

In the shallow shallows, where seaweeds sway,
Seahorses dance in a whimsical way.
With tiny top hats and monocles wide,
They twirl and they whirl, they just cannot hide!

A crab joins the party with a funky beat,
Clapping his claws in a rhythmic repeat.
Mermaids giggle, an audience grand,
As seahorses prance on the bright, golden sand.

A turtle arrives with a disco ball,
Spinning and grinning, 'You've gotta get small!'
Fish in a conga line follow along,
While everyone hums a nautical song.

With seaweed confetti and bubbles of cheer,
They dance through the currents, without any fear.
As twilight approaches, the laughs still gleam,
In the heart of the sea, we all chase a dream!

Wonders of the Harbor

Seagulls squawk like old men in the sun,
As boats doze off, their work all done.
The fish throw parties in the water, oh dear!
While barnacles sing, "We're happy here!"

The crabs compete in a dance-off spree,
While jellyfish giggle, "Look at me!"
A parrot snickers from a nearby mast,
"This harbor life is quite a blast!"

Sailboats paddle like they're in a race,
While kids build castles, smiles on each face.
The smell of fried clams fills the air so fine,
And all around, there's a coconut shrine.

So raise a toast with your soda or tea,
To the wonders that swim in life's big sea!
With laughter and joy, we're never apart,
In this quirky harbor, we find pure art.

The Siren's Call

A mermaid sings with a voice like a cat,
She lures folks in, 'cause she's quite the brat.
But instead of sailors, she gets a dog,
Who barks back, "Hey! You're stuck in a fog!"

"Oh siren sweet!" cries the gull from above,
"Your tunes need some work, they don't fit like a glove!"
The seal rolls over, laughing so loud,
While fish swim close, they'll form a crowd.

'Hey little fish, why don't you try?
Blast some bubblegum tunes as you swim by!'
The siren frowns, pulls out her old harp,
And attempts a cha-cha, it's not quite the part.

Yet everyone dances, having a ball,
Even the barnacles join the call.
So if you hear a tune that seems off the wall,
Just brush it aside, and dance after all!

Driftwood Dreams

A piece of driftwood claims to be a king,
Waving his branches, "Look at my bling!"
The seashells snicker, they've heard this song,
"Your dreams are just slivers, you don't belong!"

"King of the waves!" shouts a worn-out flip-flop,
As he twirls around, but starts to flop.
"I'll show you real jewels, from the deep blue,
They sparkle and shimmer, unlike you!"

A bottle floats by with hopes and dreams,
But it's just full of someone's old beans.
The seaweed giggles, tickling the shore,
"Let's have a party, then party some more!"

So they gather together in a sandy plot,
With laughter and tales that hit the spot.
For out on the shore, under the sun's beams,
Anything's possible in driftwood dreams!

After the Storm

The seashells gossip, wide-eyed and bright,
"Did you see the storm? What a funny sight!"
They spin little tales of waves that did dance,
And all the fish made a bid for romance.

The seagulls laugh at the washed-up debris,
"Is that a treasure or just some old sea?"
A crab tries on a lost flip-flop shoe,
"Look at me, fashion's all brand new!"

The waves crash gently, whispering laughter,
"Next time, bring popcorn for the disaster!"
The sun breaks through with a golden grin,
While dolphins flirt in a watery spin.

So let the storm come, we'll still find the cheer,
With giggles and smiles as the skies clear.
For nature's a show and we're front row seats,
After the storm, life's still full of treats!

The Language of Waves

The waves are chatting, don't you hear?
They gossip and giggle, oh so near.
A splash of laughter, a wet surprise,
As seagulls roll their feathery eyes.

They talk about fish in the ocean blue,
About all the pranks that the dolphins do.
A tidal wave of jokes, so silly and light,
Splashing our worries, making things bright.

Crabs join in, with their sideways dance,
While jellyfish wiggle, lost in a trance.
The seaweed sways, adding to the fun,
A watery party under the sun!

So next time you stand on the sandy shore,
Listen closely; there's humor galore.
The waves are gossiping, can't help but see,
Nature's stand-up, a real comedy!

Shadows in the Cove

In the cove, the shadows play,
Hiding secrets from the day.
A crab in a hat, with a wink and a nod,
Always trying to look quite odd.

Fish wearing sunglasses, oh what a sight!
Glimmering scales, they dance in the light.
A clam with a pearl, proud and aloof,
Teases the octopus, 'Come join my roof!'

A mermaid is braiding her hair with seaweed,
Laughing at sea-horses, oh what a breed!
The shadows keep chuckling, as waves crash as one,
A cove full of shadows, oh what fun!

So if you wander where the light turns dim,
You might hear a chuckle, an aquatic whim.
The shadows are dancing, just take a peek,
In the cove, they revel, with giggles they speak!

The Spirit of the Lighthouse

Up high in the lighthouse, what do we see?
A ghost with a lantern, not scary, but free!
He shines a bright light, to guide the lost,
But tells bad jokes, at a very high cost.

Nautical puns, oh what a delight,
He laughs at the ships that pass through the night.
A sailor gets tangled in his own net,
The ghost chuckles softly, 'That's a safe bet!'

Seagulls are cawing, rolling their eyes,
At the ghost in the tower, oh what a surprise!
'You're supposed to be scary, instead, you're a hoot!'
But the ghost just keeps telling his jokes, to boot.

So if you see lights that flicker and gleam,
It might just be him, living the dream.
The spirit of fun, with jokes up his sleeve,
Bringing joy to the night, oh, we believe!

Gentle Ripples

Gentle ripples dance on the sea,
Smiling at boats as they sail so free.
A duck wearing shades floats by with flair,
Quacking out tunes, without a care.

The fish in the water start to groove,
Bouncing about, they're in the mood.
A crab with a conga, moves to the beat,
His tiny claws tapping, oh so neat!

Sunsets bring colors, both bold and bright,
While the waves whisper softly, 'Everything's right.'
A dolphin dives deep with a splash and a giggle,
Causing a starfish to wiggle and jiggle.

So let's enjoy this watery scene,
A world full of laughter, where everyone's keen.
The gentle ripples remind us each day,
To take life lightly, and play in the spray!

Secrets Beneath the Surf

A crab in a tuxedo dances with flair,
While the fish flash their scales with a debonair air.
Jellyfish juggle, all wobbly and grand,
Making waves of laughter with just a quick hand.

Seahorses gossip in underwater chat,
About that one octopus, donning a hat.
Clams snap their shells, but it's all in good fun,
They hide all their pearls from the sun's golden run.

Starfish play poker, no bluffing aloud,
While seaweed provides quite the comfy crowd.
Dolphins surf bubbles, a splashy delight,
Cheering on turtles who take flying flights.

Bubbles rise up, and a hermit crab grins,
Counting all the shells that his collection spins.
With laughter and joy as they frolic and play,
Beneath all the waters, they brightened the day.

Horizons of Blue

Paddling penguins in shades just for kicks,
Wobble and tumble do acrobatic tricks.
Their beach ball goes flying, splashing with glee,
While seagulls take bets on who'll land in the sea.

A walrus in workout gear flexes with pride,
Claiming he lifts boats as he floats on the tide.
Fish gossip around, oh, the tales they can weave,
About mermaids who moonwalk and twirl on their leaves.

A lighthouse sings ballads to the passing ships,
While crabs shake their claws and join in with the flips.
With waves rolling in, there's a splash-tastic cheer,
As everyone joins in, feeling free from all fear.

Turtles take selfies, they pose with a twist,
Making sure to capture each glorious gist.
The sun sets in colors that shimmer and shine,
With laughter and fun as they all intertwine.

Where Waves Kiss the Shore

A seal takes a selfie, struck by its charm,
Flipping and flapping, it means no harm.
The sand's in a tangle, as feet start to dance,
With crabs holding hands, oh, what a romance!

Seashells tell stories in whispers so sweet,
Of pirates and treasure, oh, what a treat!
A sandcastle towers, adorned with a flag,
But a wise seagull swoops down for a brag.

A beach ball rolls past, chased down by a pup,
Who pounces and tumbles, then gives it a sup.
The tide laughs along as it pulls back away,
Leaving behind footprints that shimmer and play.

With laughter shared freely, they lie on the sand,
Making memories cherished, a whimsical band.
The fun never ends when the sun's shining bright,
As waves kiss the shore with pure, joyous delight.

Salty Serenade

A clam with a kazoo leads a merry parade,
While starfish applaud with their arms all displayed.
The dolphins burst forth, doing flips in the sun,
With songs and with laughter, oh, isn't this fun?

A school of fish grooving to rhythm and beat,
Twirl around seaweed, on their vibrant retreat.
The octopus winks, adorning a bow,
While turtles decide it's time to throw down.

With a splash and a giggle, the sea critters sway,
As the rhythm of waves leads them all into play.
A sea cucumber joins, with the best of intentions,
In a dance-off of colors, the fanciest inventions.

So grab all your friends, and let spirits soar,
With shells full of laughter, who could ask for more?
Singing sea shanties beneath the blue sky,
As the salty serenade makes the worries fly.

A Moment at Water's Breath

Splashing waves with a flip-flop,
Caught in tides, it's a wild hop.
Seagulls squawking, what a show,
As I chase them, oh, the woe.

Sunburned backs and sand-filled shoes,
Laughter echoes, take your views.
Friends diving in, but one runs late,
Trips on seaweed, oh, what fate!

Ice cream melts in the sunny glare,
Sticky fingers, but we don't care.
Seashell treasures, one I found,
Turns out it's a long-lost hound!

With each wave, a laugh we share,
Belly flops and salty hair.
A day of fun, and what's more,
I dare you—try to keep the score!

Shores of Endless Reflection

Footprints left in a sandy maze,
Who knew I'd start my clumsy phase?
Jumping waves, then losing track,
Right back down, oh what a whack!

My beach ball flew, straight to a crab,
It waved its claws, oh how it drab!
Chasing it down, but what a tease,
I trip again, can't catch the breeze!

Sun hats flew as the wind did play,
Sandy snacks left in disarray.
Find a towel, take a seat—whoops!
Drenched again by playful loops!

As the sun bids goodnight, we grin,
Salt and sand, that's how we win.
Share the tales of this crazy day,
We'll laugh again—come what may!

The Horizon's Veil

Chasing shadows through the spray,
I swear this fish just said 'Hey!'
A surfboard flips, and off I go,
Thought I had skills, but not a show.

Seashells whisper tales so grand,
But most just grin at my awkward stand.
Pretending to paddle, I look so tough,
Turns out the waves just call my bluff!

Kites soar high, then come down low,
A chase ensues, oh what a show.
Tangled strings and laughter loud,
In this silly space, I'm so proud!

A splash here, a splash there,
Nobody's dry, not one to spare.
With laughs and cheers, our hearts will tell,
Of sandy antics, we've done so well!

Secrets of the Surf

What's in the waves? I must know,
A stray flip-flop's on the go.
A crab in shades—who wears them best?
This beach life surely beats the rest!

I saw a dolphin dance, it's true,
But it laughed at me—what's my cue?
Pretending to surf, I ride a wave,
And end up just a little knave!

Seashell fashion, quite the sight,
Oh look, I've got a clam tonight!
Footsteps wrong, I stroll with flair,
Barefoot antics lead to a stare!

As the sun waves its goodbye,
I'll tell my tales, oh me, oh my!
With laughter ringing, our hearts align,
In salty air, life's just divine!

www.ingramcontent.com/pod-product-compliance
Lightning Source LLC
Chambersburg PA
CBHW072222070526
44585CB00015B/1457